1 MONTH FREE READING

at

www.ForgottenBooks.com

By purchasing this book you are eligible for one month membership to ForgottenBooks.com, giving you unlimited access to our entire collection of over 1,000,000 titles via our web site and mobile apps.

To claim your free month visit:

www.forgottenbooks.com/free302965

English
Français
Deutsche
Italiano
Español
Português

www.forgottenbooks.com

Mythology Photography **Fiction**
Fishing Christianity **Art** Cooking
Essays Buddhism Freemasonry
Medicine **Biology** Music **Ancient**
Egypt Evolution Carpentry Physics
Dance Geology **Mathematics** Fitness
Shakespeare **Folklore** Yoga Marketing
Confidence Immortality Biographies
Poetry **Psychology** Witchcraft
Electronics Chemistry History **Law**
Accounting **Philosophy** Anthropology
Alchemy Drama Quantum Mechanics
Atheism Sexual Health **Ancient History**
Entrepreneurship Languages Sport
Paleontology Needlework Islam
Metaphysics Investment Archaeology
Parenting Statistics Criminology
Motivational

ISBN 978-1-332-24073-9
PIBN 10302965

This book is a reproduction of an important historical work. Forgotten Books uses state-of-the-art technology to digitally reconstruct the work, preserving the original format whilst repairing imperfections present in the aged copy. In rare cases, an imperfection in the original, such as a blemish or missing page, may be replicated in our edition. We do, however, repair the vast majority of imperfections successfully; any imperfections that remain are intentionally left to preserve the state of such historical works.

American Civic Association

DEPARTMENT OF NUISANCES

SERIES II, NO. 1   MARCH, 1908

Second Edition, February, 1911

THE
SMOKE NUISANCE

BY

FREDERICK LAW OLMSTED

HARLAN PAGE KELSEY

AND THE OFFICERS OF THE ASSOCIATION

"*The way to abate smoke is not to make it.*"

"*All who are guilty of polluting the atmosphere should be penalized. New York City makes a practice of this and has the most effective smoke-prevention ordinance in the land.*"

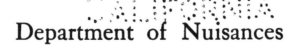

Department of Nuisances

(Address all general communications to the AMERICAN CIVIC ASSOCIATION, Union Trust Building, Washington, D. C.

CONTENTS

J. Horace McFarland Company, Harrisburg, Pa.

THE SMOKE NUISANCE

INTRODUCTION

The second pamphlet issued by the American Civic Association after its organization in 1904 was one dealing with the smoke nuisance prepared by Frederick Law Olmsted, Jr., of Brookline, Massachusetts. It has had a wide circulation and has proved a most useful statement of fundamental principles. A number of editions have been called for. Since its publication, however, there has been a very great and encouraging development of public sentiment in the question and a corresponding demand for information and concrete suggestions. This present pamphlet is intended to meet that need. As R. C. Harris, Property Commissioner of Toronto, said, "I believe that an interchange of ideas, and a tendency toward uniform legislation, will greatly assist in the remedy of this public nuisance."

The present pamphlet is intended to provide this interchange of ideas and to promote a tendency towards uniform legislation, and generally to create an intelligent public opinion on the smoke nuisance and to indicate measures of effective remedy.

The pamphlet contains Mr. Olmsted's original leaflet brought up to date, with references to the recent statutes and ordinances. It also contains the helpful paper of Mr. George W. Welden, of the New York, New Haven & Hartford Railroad, on "The Smoke Nuisance on Railroad Locomotives," which paper was read at the Providence meeting of the American Civic Association in November, 1907; also the larger part of Paul M. Chamberlain's paper on "Boiler Room Economy," delivered before the Milwaukee meeting of the International Association for the Abatement of the Smoke Nuisance.*

Members of the Association and others interested in this work will find the recent pamphlet prepared by D. T. Randall, issued by the Federal Government through the Geological Survey, and the pamphlet by Prof. L. P. Breckenridge, on "How to Burn Soft Coal Without Smoke," issued by the University of Illinois, extremely useful documents.

*"The Smoke Nuisance and the Law," in the present edition, brings the legal phase up to 1911.

270345

1. THE NUISANCE

The dweller in a town burning bituminous coal needs no definition of the smoke nuisance. The great cloud that hangs over the city like a pall can be seen from any neighboring hill-top, and the dweller within is only too well aware of the splotches of soot that settle on every object in the city, bedimming buildings, spoiling curtains, injuring books, and increasing the laundry bill. The direct menace to the public health in fostering tuberculous conditions by loading the air with carbon particles to lodge in the lungs, and by causing house-keepers to keep the windows shut for fear of the soot that floats in when they are open, is equaled only by the mentally and physically depressing effect of the pall which shuts out the life-giving and germ-destroying sunshine. Our city parks have mostly lost their evergreen character, where it existed, as conifers cannot long endure city smoke. Thus one treatment of the most pleasing variations in landscape is made impossible.

Dr. George M. Goler, health officer of Rochester, New York, in a paper read before the American Civic Association and National Municipal League at Providence, Rhode Island, November, 1907, says:

"The old saying 'free as air,' so often quoted, should in cities be changed to 'as dear as air.' The poor man or poor woman, compelled to live near the middle of the city, must necessarily breathe smoke-polluted air. This smoke-polluted air attacks the organs of the bodies, chiefly the lungs. The poor man cannot afford to go to the suburbs to breathe smoke-less air. He must live in the center of the city. When he suffers from lung disease, the doctor prescribes what he cannot afford to have,—pure air.

"As an example, we show the following table of suspected lung diseases for a period of years. From 1895 to 1904 the number of cases of suspected lung disease *increased with the increase of the smoke nuisance*, and was highest during the year of the coal strike. The use of bituminous coal under boilers that are improperly fired creates smoke that means disease, uncleanliness, poverty, death and wretchedness.

"Examination for diphtheria and tuberculosis: 1895, 756; 1900, 1,188: 1903, 2,613; 1905, 2,692; 1906, 2,731; 1907, 1,825."*

The poet Shelley describes the capital of the nether world as

*Estimated for 1907.

"A city much like London—
A populous and a smoky city."

Prof. C. Roberts recently estimated the canopy daily over-shadowing London as fifty tons of solid carbon, and two hundred and fifty tons of carbonic oxide gas, acids and hydro-carbons, and its black fogs are proved to be caused largely by the smoke issuing from its vast forest of chimneys. London, however, is at last realizing the frightful price its• people are paying in sickness, disease, death and a yearly economic loss, estimated at £4,000,000, for such so-called evidences of "ma-terial prosperity," and is with increasing rapidity and effective-ness doing away with this, perhaps its greatest of all public nuisances. Our American cities, too, are at last awakening, and are seeing the new light of a brighter, clearer, smokeless day. Where once belching chimneys, soot-laden air, clanging noises and landscape blighted with flaming billboards and ten thousand intruding poles and wires were considered signs of municipal "push," prosperity and business health, such evidences are now rightly more often termed municipal igno-rance, crime, and business gangrene.

2. ITS ABATEMENT

There should be complete understanding of the scientific fact that visible black smoke is made up almost entirely of un-consumed particles of combustible carbon, or coal, wasted into the atmosphere through imperfect combustion. It is economic waste, in itself; and its emission creates additional waste.

No really intelligent person now denies the imperative economic and sanitary need for abating or suppressing the smoke evil, nor the feasibility and absolute power of existing authori-ties to do so where the will and proper public sentiment exist.

The tearing down of a dangerous house, the draining of a pestiferous swamp, the cleaning of a filthy street, or of a back yard, are simple remedies for simple nuisances. The abolition of smoke, on the other hand, affects the whole community, since the production of smoke is claimed, especially by the careless or the uninformed, to be completely bound up with the material and industrial welfare of a city. The evil is one that grows with the growth of the community, and its abate-ment calls for a large, comprehensive and tactful treatment, with thorough coöperation between the different parties to the problem. Education of the public, the factory owners and the firemen to the bad economy and the wrong of smoke emission is of great importance.

The smoke nuisance can be abated either by right stoking and furnaces insuring proper combustion of smoky fuels, or by substituting a smokeless fuel. The latter, especially in large steam plants, may not be possible from an economical standpoint, when the smoky fuel is materially cheaper than the smokeless fuel.

The other remedy—proper combustion—is a matter of taking the pains to burn the coal or other material properly, and it can be substantially accomplished wherever people realize that the result is worth the trouble necessary to secure it.

The first step in abating smoke is to pass a law or an ordinance, making the emission of black or dark gray smoke an unlawful act, punishable by fine. Such regulations are already in force in New York, Cleveland, Milwaukee, Toronto, Toledo, Indianapolis, Detroit, the District of Columbia, and numerous other cities. The second step is to get the law enforced. This may be done by a smoke-abatement department, or, as in some cities, by the health department. In any case, the work should be done under the direction of smoke inspectors' or officers delegated for the purpose, who understand boilers and their construction, and whose chief duty is to *see that the smoke is abated.* It is purely a question of engineering, and any manufacturer or others may readily obtain expert aid that will enable him to comply with the law. A part of the work of the official might well be in educating both the public and the coal consumer in the actual economic advantages of perfect combustion and consequent freedom from smoke.

The actual means employed to abate any specific smoking chimney must necessarily depend on local conditions. The kind of fuel, the kind of service, the size of the plant, the character of labor, the variation in load, the strength of the fire, are some of the determining factors. The problem to be solved is to get the comparatively cool, smoky, gaseous product, given off from cold fuel when applied to a hot fire, so mixed with air and so heated that its proper combustion will be secured. This result, in some cases, may best be obtained by careful and frequent hand-firing; in others, by mechanical stokers, which feed the fuel so slowly, regularly and evenly that the volatile gases are distilled off gradually, and mixed with air sufficient to insure their perfect combustion in the hotter parts of the furnace. In other plants, the introduction of steam jets in such positions that they act during the firing of the furnace as conveyers and mixers of a larger air-supply, offers a solution. Other devices, including down-draft furnaces, gas-generating furnaces, under-feed furnaces, furnaces for burning powdered coal, and furnaces using oil as an auxiliary heater, have been successfully applied under certain conditions.

In every case, *smoke is a preventable nuisance*, and every smoking plant or locomotive is a sign of wastefulness, and a disregard for the rights of the public. The proprietor should be as interested in abating the nuisance as his neighbors, and it has been the experience of smoke-law officials that men who have bitterly complained at being forced to make improvements have afterward thanked the smoke-abating department for the increased economy of the plant.

BOILER ROOM ECONOMY

Extract from an illustrated lecture delivered before the International Association for the Prevention of Smoke, Milwaukee, Wis., June 26, 1907, by Paul M. Chamberlain, of Chicago.

A SAVING AT THE BOILER WILL PRODUCE A DIRECT SAVING.

As the problem of increased savings presents itself to us, is it not strange that so much of the thought, expense and experiment should have been put on the engine end? Assuming the case of apparatus having an output of 50% of the heat value of the coal, and the engine and condenser an efficiency of 14% (corresponding to 18 pounds of steam per H. P.), an increase of efficiency of the engine to 27% (probably the limit) would mean only a saving of half the difference between 14% and 27%, or 6½%. A saving at the boiler end will produce a direct saving. The nearer to the original source of power we get the saving, the more intact is our efficiency. This takes us back to the burning of the coal, and it is with this problem that this association is most vitally concerned. We use the term "efficiency" here in the sense of ratio of energy gotten out to energy supplied. The efficient burning of coal is very closely related to smokeless combustion. The theory of complete and smokeless combustion is very simple in statement, and the statement of conditions under which it will take place is equally simple. Coal is composed, for the most part, of fixed carbon, volatile matter, moisture and ash. As the great majority of steam plants employ bituminous

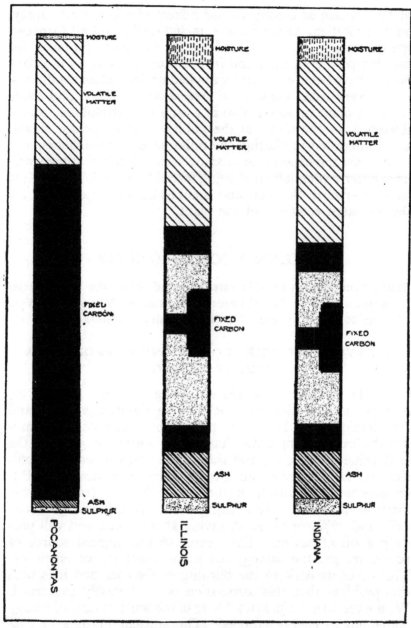

Fig. 1. Composition of various bituminous coals.

coal, we shall consider only it. Fig. 1 will show approximately the proportions of the various constituents.

The bituminous coal which gives the least trouble with smoke is that found in Virginia and West Virginia, usually spoken of as Pocahontas. This coal contains a very small proportion of ash and volatile matter, while the carbon is about three-quarters of the whole. In the Indiana and Illinois coals the ash and volatile matter are high, and fixed carbon less than half the total.

THE THEORY OF COMBUSTION

The burning of coal is accomplished by bringing the oxygen of the air into intimate contact with the combustible elements under proper conditions of temperature. In the calorimeter we get the total heat from coal by using oxygen under pressure, and a perfect mixture ensues, giving the desired chemical combination. In the furnace good combustion is accomplished in the following manner:

The fixed or free carbon left in the form of coke, when the volatile matter has been driven off, burns as solid matter, the carbon combining with oxygen in the ratio of one part of carbon to two of oxygen, forming carbon dioxide, CO_2.

The volatile matter or hydrocarbons must first pass into a gaseous state and mix thoroughly with hot air, forming CO_2, and hydrogen which combines with oxygen and forms water in the condition of steam due to the high temperature.

HOW INCOMPLETE COMBUSTION OCCURS

Incomplete combustion would take place first, by insufficient or incomplete mixture of air, allowing the CO_2 from the coke to take on more carbon, giving 2 CO. Second, the hydrocarbons mixed with cold air pass off unconsumed, or if raised to a red heat and without sufficient air disengage carbon in fine powder and pass to the condition of marsh gas and hydrogen. The *higher* the temperature under the conditions of insufficient air, the greater the proportion of carbon powder. *If the carbon powder is cooled below the temperature of ignition before coming in contact with oxygen, it passes off as smoke.*

REQUIREMENTS FOR COMPLETE COMBUSTION

For complete combustion it is necessary to have not only sufficient air, but intimately mixed at the right place and temperature with the burning carbon and volatile matter. Too much air is a detriment because it absorbs the heat and acts to some extent as an insulator between the hot gases and the heating surface.

NECESSITY OF PROPER SUPPLY OF AIR

The ideal conditions are to have at all times the proper supply of air intimately mixed with the burning carbon and volatile matter gases, and a combustion or mixing chamber large enough to allow each particle of carbon to get its necessary oxygen at the required temperature for combination.

To correct as far as possible the lack of ideal conditions,

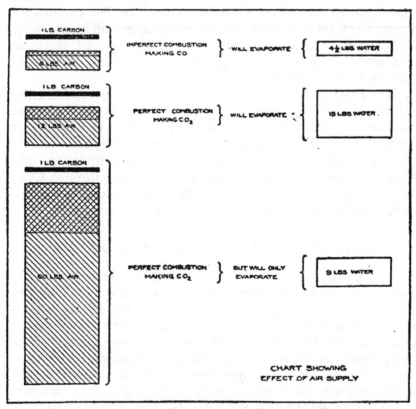

Fig. 2. Relations of air supply to combustion and efficiency.

many expedients are resorted to, such as brick arches over the fire, mixing piers and steam jets, all with the object of getting the hydrocarbons from the volatile matter in intimate mixture with air at the proper temperature for ignition.

A simple, ordinary furnace, with proper chimney, proper grade of coal, and skillful firing for uniform demand of steam, will give satisfactory combustion. The failure of economic and smokeless combustion in such plants may occur from any one of three causes: The proper coal may not be available or economical; the demand for steam may vary beyond the capacity of either chimney or fireman to meet satisfactorily; the skillful fireman is likely to get a better job. These three failures have been variously met: Chimneys capable of handling the maximum duty; with dampers for the lighter loads; induced draft by fans; and again the use of blowers to supply the required air with sufficient chimney to carry off the prod-

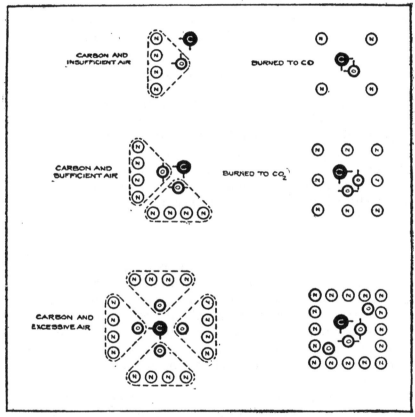

Fig. 3. Chemical results of combustion.

ncts of combustion; the high degree of skill required on the part of the hand fireman has been modified by the invention of various mechanical stokers which will handle poorer grades of coal; the variable load duty has been met by automatic supply of coal and air, both controlled by the steam pressure.

If a pound of carbon is burned to carbon monoxide, or CO, it will give off 4,400 B. T. U., or sufficient heat to evaporate 4.55 pounds of water. If it is burned to carbon dioxide, or CO_2, it will produce 14,500 B. T. U., or evaporate 15 pounds of water. If 500% of air be supplied, the pound of carbon will evaporate only 9.3 pounds of water. This is illustrated graphically by Fig. 2.

The chemical combination of carbon with oxygen may be imagined as taking place as shown in Fig. 3. The oxygen is furnished by the air in a mixture with nitrogen—four parts of nitrogen to one of oxygen. The atom of carbon can combine with one atom of oxygen, setting free four atoms of nitrogen, forming CO, or with two atoms of oxygen forming CO_2. If there is excess air, the flue gases will have free oxygen and much nitrogen to take up heat and dilute the temperature.

REGARDING LOSSES

Some losses to the stack are unavoidable even with perfect combustion. The transfer of heat to the boiler from the gases is proportionate in speed to the difference of temperature between the gases and the water. As steam at 100 pounds pressure has a temperature of 388°, it is apparent that the flue temperature must not be much below 400° to get any considerable effect from the heating surface in contact with the gases near their exit.

In addition to the unavoidable loss, there may be much CO and other gases carrying away fuel value due to insufficient air, incomplete mixture, or lack of proper temperature.

The chimney may also carry off much heat from excess of air. Every four pounds of air passing up the chimney carries away heat enough to evaporate about one pound of water.

The loss due to too much air through or over the fire is frequently augmented by leakage through the brick work. The heat wasted by radiation can be reduced somewhat by insulating coverings.

The moisture in coal must have heat to evaporate it and for every pound of water evaporated in the furnace there is heat enough absorbed to have evaporated an equal amount in the boiler.

THE SMOKE ABATEMENT QUESTION

How can the smoke be abated and the economy increased? In the light of the foregoing discussion, it is obvious that the one thing needed is more complete combustion. A clear-headed smoke doctor is needed in every municipality, who is capable of examining the conditions unprejudicedly and prescribing the proper remedy. To make this doctor's services of value, there must be laws suited to force unwilling offenders to mend their ways.

In looking for causes of insufficient and smoky operation, the following questions should be considered:

1. Is the boiler being forced beyond its capacity?
2. Is there sufficient chimney capacity?
3. Is there room in furnace and combustion chamber for proper mixture of air and gases before the gases are cooled?

Relative to crowding the boiler: The rating is usually known, or, if not, can be computed by measuring the square feet of heating surface and dividing by ten for fire tube boilers or by twelve for return flue boilers to get the horse-power rating. The horse-power that is being developed can be ascertained by an evaporating test, weighing water and allowing thirty-four and a half pounds of water per hour to the horse-power, on the basis of the water being evaporated from and at 212° Fahr. A general idea of the horse-power being developed can be had by weighing the coal for an hour, or weighing a barrowful or shovelful and noting the amount fired in an hour. Many inefficient plants burn as much as five pounds of coal per horse-power per hour; dividing by five would give some idea of the horse-power being developed.

The question of chimney capacity, superficially investigated, can be observed by taking a glass "U" tube and getting the draft in the furnace. If there is found as low as one-quarter inch of water under hand-fired conditions, the probability is that there is insufficient draft.

The question of the proper combustion space is more difficult to define. If the boiler is not running with too much over-load, with sufficient draft, and there is smoke, then the presumption is that there is too little combustion space for hand-firing. The space between the grate and the boiler is in most cases too small for smokelessness with hand firing.

The many careful observations necessary to arrive at definite conclusions are too complicated for discussion in this address, and any specific problem should be referred to men or firms whose reputation assures competence to handle the combustion problem.

PROPER HAND-FIRING*

In previous sections of this report it has been seen that, in American cities, most dependence in the matter of smoke-

*Extracts from Section IV of the Syracuse 1907 Report.

abatement is put upon mechanical devices. Quite the opposite seems to be true in Great Britain and on the Continent, where much attention is paid to proper methods of hand-firing, and where schools are, in some places, maintained for the instruction of firemen. The English Coal Smoke-Abatement Society, some years ago, addressed a number of firms which had been successful in abating smoke, and, of thirty-five satisfactory replies, thirteen ascribe their success to *careful stoking*, and the replies, as a whole, demonstrate that, while not denying the efficacy of many mechanical devices, the consensus of opinion favors skillful and careful stoking as of first importance.

It is obvious that the proper training of firemen has been sadly neglected. An intelligent fireman is worthy of good pay, but many of them, doubtless, waste more than their wages daily because of either ignorance or carelessness in handling their furnaces. This is especially true in small plants, and small plants preponderate in every city, and in these plants the possibility of great economies through the installation of mechanical stokers is small. Yet firemen can hardly be expected to know intuitively the chemistry of combustion, and certain it is that they have never been instructed in the fundamental principles of their occupation. Muscle and endurance have been considered the chief elements in the make-up of a fireman, and the arduous duties, too often performed in dark, hot and ill-ventilated basements, have not attracted many men of intelligence.

In St. Louis, the Smoke-Abatement Department causes to be posted in every boiler-room a list of "Directions for Firing." These are intended, primarily, for the users of low-pressure steam-heating plants, in which no mechanical device has, as yet, proven perfectly satisfactory. In such plants, especially, and in all other hand-firing boilers, efficiency is improved, and smoke may be greatly lessened by close adherence to the following rules:

1. Fire frequently, in small quantities, and at regular intervals.

2. Break up lumps to fist-size.

3. Carry a level surface over entire grate.

4. Avoid thin and bare spots on grate.

5. Keep the fires clean.

6. Fire one door at a time, and wait until that fire is in good shape before charging the other door.

7. Leave furnace door slightly ajar for one minute after each firing.

The Laundrymen's Association finds an average increase of two collars a week laundered for each patron last year.

GUIDE.—"Here is Statistics Sammy. He's great on figures. He has a scheme now to build a new city hall without expense.

SAMMY.—"How? Extremely simple! By referring to my figures you will see that by stopping some of the smoke, the taxpayers, who wear collars, could wear them longer and save at least four cents each per week at no expense to anybody, and in five years—

"but just a minute! I'll show you how Chicago could pay for the Panama Canal without feeling it, if all the smoke was stopped."

—Chicago Record-Herald

3. SUCCESSFUL SMOKE LAWS AND ORDINANCES AND HOW THEY ARE ENFORCED*

NEW YORK CITY

The smoke nuisance has been successfully abated in New York City. The sanitary code of the Board of Health provides that: "No person shall cause, suffer or allow dense smoke to be discharged from any building, vessel, stationary or locomotive engine, place or premises, within the city of New York, or upon the waters adjacent thereto, within the jurisdiction of said city. All persons participating in any violation of this provision, either as proprietors, owners, tenants, managers, superintendents, captains, engineers, firemen, or otherwise, shall be severally liable therefor."

Under this law, Judge Fawcett imposed on the Transit Development Company, a subsidiary concern of the Brooklyn Rapid Transit Company, a fine of $500 on November 1, 1907. This company is completely readjusting its plant in compliance with the law. Health Commissioner Thomas Darlington has expressed his opinion, and that of the Health Board, that the ordinance is, on the whole, most satisfactory.

SPRINGFIELD, MASS.

Chapter 236, Acts of 1900, Commonwealth of Massachusetts, is "An act to abate the smoke nuisance in the city of Springfield."

William T. Gale, City Forester, in charge of the abatement of smoke in Springfield, November 29, 1907, is authority for the statement: "Springfield has been quite successful; and I think that we are the cleanest city of 80,000 population in New England,—at least so far as smoke goes. The Boston & Albany railway, and a few of the larger concerns, have given us some trouble. I brought suits in 1906 against the gas company, three breweries, and two railway heating plants, which resulted in their being fined $50 each. This year I have had all the railroads, one brewery (second case), and the street railway in court, all but the last being fined $50, and the street railway company $150."

*Copies of the laws and ordinances herein mentioned may be obtained by addressing the proper authorities.

DISTRICT OF COLUMBIA

An Act of Congress for the prevention of smoke in the District of Columbia, and for other purposes, was passed in 1899. Here is a summary of the smoke inspector's last annual report:

```
Violations of law reported ...................906
Cases referred to corporation counsel ........ 72
Cases in which fines or forfeitures were paid .. 64
Cases in which personal bonds were taken....   2
Cases acquitted ...........................   1
Cases pending ............................  14
Amount of fines and forfeitures paid ..... $1,615
```

One inspector is at work all the time enforcing this law. In practice, prosecutions are based on emissions lasting one minute or more, and a prosecution is instituted for every emission lasting more than a minute.

WILLIAM C. WOODWARD, Health Officer,
District of Columbia, December 4, 1907.

DENVER, COLORADO

"During the year 1907, there were $60,000 worth of equipment installed in Denver, principally in mechanical stokers, and they are giving good results. The outlook is good here."

PHIL McCARTY, City Boiler and Smoke Inspector,
Denver, December 5, 1907.

CLEVELAND, OHIO

Ordinance No. 41,586, approved June 4, 1903, is "An ordinance to prevent the emission of dense, black or gray smoke from smoke-stacks, chimneys, locomotive engines, and all other smoke-emitting stacks."

Cleveland is one of the few cities which are really suppressing locomotive smoke. According to John Krause, supervising engineer, "50 per cent of the smoke in Cleveland has been abated since this department was organized."

MILWAUKEE, WIS.

Chapter 21 of the general ordinances of the city of Milwaukee, passed May 28, 1906, as amended, is the law.

"In 1906, after the passage of the present ordinance, I had

seven cases, viz., two tanning concerns, one railroad, one packing company, one harvester company, and two manufacturing concerns. In 1907, there were, up to this date, fifty-two cases, consisting of railroad companies, packing houses, tanneries, breweries, malt houses, flour mills, planing mills, coal companies, river dredges, flat buildings, and various other manufacturing establishments.

"Ninety-nine smoke-preventing devices were installed during the year. These comprise three classes of stokers, the down-draft furnaces, and the automatic steam and air-jet systems, as follows:

"Underfeed stokers 32
Traveling, or chain-grate stoker 2
Inclined grate stoker 15
Down-draft furnaces 6
Automatic steam and air-jet systems ...44

"The manufacturers have, as a rule, shown a willingness to coöperate with the work of abating the smoke nuisance."

CHARLES POETHKE, Smoke Inspector,
Milwaukee, November 20, 1907.

PHILADELPHIA, PA.

Smoke ordinance, approved December 9, 1904, amended April 3, 1906.

"During the year 1906, there have been 1,945 investigations made and reports entered in this office by the smoke inspectors. Sixty-two firms have abated the smoke nuisance. We are now bringing action against the offenders in this city, and find that in the majority of cases when action is brought they are very ready to go out into the market and secure some appliance for the abatement of the nuisance."

Annual Report Bureau of Steam Engine and Boiler Inspection,

JOHN M. LUKENS, Chief Inspector.

TORONTO, CANADA

No. 4,266. A by-law to compel manufacturers and others creating smoke to use smoke consumers, passed October 5, 1903.

"Our laws do not permit of the abatement of a fine once imposed. We have found that the prosecution aforementioned has accomplished a very great deal of good, and that the people who formerly treated the enactment very lightly, are now making sincere efforts to comply with same."

R. C. HARRIS, Property Commissioner,
Toronto, December 2, 1907.

PROVIDENCE, R. I.

"There are plants in this city that formerly were large smoke producers, and, in all probability, would still continue so, but for changes made in the engineering department by employing more progressive and intelligent help, who have made a very satisfactory showing as to smoke issue, and materially diminished the coal bills. Firemen who can be hired for eight dollars a week, as in some of our large establishments, cannot be expected to be found very proficient in the art of stoking."

H. E. CHADWICK, Supervising Engineer, January 1, 1907.

PITTSBURG, PA.

"The coöperation on the part of the general public has been remarkable. Not one person of all those visited has refused to take some action toward eliminating the smoke. The active force engaged on this work, as you will see by the ordinance, consists of a chief smoke inspector, and four deputies."

WM. H. REA, Smoke Inspector,
Department of Public Safety, November 20, 1907.

It is generally admitted that Pittsburg is less smoky than formerly, which is a notably hopeful condition.

CINCINNATI, OHIO

"Our report to the mayor for this year will show a list of over one hundred plants improved, which will be about ten per cent of the whole number of plants in the city."

GEORGE SEALEY, Chief Smoke Inspector, November 20, 1907.

The following cities also have smoke ordinances: Buffalo, N. Y.; Rochester, N. Y.; Syracuse, N. Y.; Grand Rapids, Mich.; Reading, Pa.; Minneapolis; St. Louis; Boston; Dayton, Ohio; Kansas City, Mo.; Detroit; Hamilton, Canada.

—Chicago Tribune

4. THE SMOKE NUISANCE AND THE LAW

By CYRUS LOCHER, ESQ., of the Cleveland Chamber of Commerce*

With the beginning of the use of soft coal as a fuel arose the problem of how to get rid of the resulting smoke. The problem has grown more serious every year in every growing city where a large quantity of bituminous coal is consumed, and the dweller in the town burning bituminous coal needs no definition of the smoke nuisance.

It has become a matter of vital importance to every large city to rid itself as far as possible of smoke; and that interest in the question is widespread and fully aroused, is attested by the many methods devised for the suppression of the nuisance and the legislation enacted in all the jurisdictions where bituminous coal is the chief fuel. More than 1,500 patents have been granted by the United States Bureau to inventors of so-called "smoke consumers" and "smoke burners," and everywhere municipal governments have taken up seriously the abating of the smoke nuisance. But it does not require the testimony of an expert to convince one that the smoke nuisance has by no means been satisfactorily abated.

That objectional smoke may be prevented has been demonstrated by experience, although, soft or bituminous coal may be used exclusively as fuel, first, by careful firing, either by hand or the employment of a mechanical stoker or feeder, resulting in a uniform distribution of fresh coal on the hot furnace bed; second, by mechanical appliances designed to perfect the draught and cause a sufficient uniform degree of heat to reach all parts of the coal, and thus avoid a "smothering" producing that lower degree of heat favorable to the separation of the material which makes smoke from the body of the coal. Sometimes an entirely new furnace equipment is the only remedy.

Smoke abatement, which is simply complete combustion and utilization of all heat-producing parts of the coal, is economy to the consumer of fuel. In every case smoke is a preventable nuisance, and every smoking plant or locomotive is a sign of wastefulness and a disregard for the rights of the public. Creating dense smoke is a waste in itself, and its emission creates additional waste. Thus it follows that the interests of the private

*Read before the Washington meeting of the American Civic Association, December 13, 1910.

owner and the public health, comfort and convenience run in parallel lines.

Proper laws for the regulation, prevention and abatement of "dense" smoke are, therefore, just to the consumer of fuel and highly desirable to the public.

And I am called upon to discuss some of the fundamental principles of the law pertaining to the prevention of the smoke evil, rather than indulge in a discussion of the abatement of smoke from an engineering standpoint.

The source of power of governmental authority to abate the smoke nuisance is the police power of the state. "The powers not delegated to the United States by the constitution, nor prohibited by it to the states, are reserved to the states respectively, or to the people."[1] The police power is inherent in the several states, and is left with them under the federal system of government, and may always be exercised by the state legislatures.[2] The federal government can exercise police power only where the authority of Congress excludes territorially all state legislation, as, for instance, in the District of Columbia, where the police power of Congress is the same as that of the state legislatures within their several jurisdictions.[3] The police power inherent in the states is not derived from the constitutions of the several states, which merely apportion and impose restrictions upon the powers which the states inherently possess, and in the American constitutional system this power left with the individual states cannot be taken from them, either wholly or in part.

WHAT IS THE POLICE POWER?—It is inadvisable to attempt to form any definition of the police power which absolutely indicates its limits by including everything to which it may extend and excluding everything to which it cannot extend. The courts have considered it better to decide each case arising whether the police power extends thereto. Many definitions, however, have been attempted in a general way, and the sum of these definitions is, that the police power in its broadest acceptation means the general power of the government to preserve and promote the public welfare by prohibiting all things hurtful to the

[1] Constitution U. S., Art. X.
[2] Munn vs. Ill., 94 M. S. 113; Arnold vs. Yarders, 56 Ohio State 417.
[3] Mases vs. U. S., 16 App. Cas. (D. C.) 428; Civil Rights Cases, 109 M. S. 3.

comfort, safety and welfare of society and establishing such rules and regulations for the conduct of all persons and the use and management of all property as may be conducive to the public interest.[1] In a comprehensive sense it embraces the state's whole system of internal regulation by which the states seek not only to preserve the public order and to prevent offenses against the state, but also to establish for the intercourse of citizens those rules which are calculated to prevent a conflict of right, to insure to each the uninterrupted enjoyment of his own as far as is reasonable and consistent with a like enjoyment of the rights of others.[2] It is universally conceded that the extent and limits of the police power include everything essential to the public safety, health and convenience of the public and to justify the abatement by summary proceedings of whatever may be regarded as a public nuisance.[3]

The legislature, however, has no right arbitrarily to declare that to be a nuisance which is clearly not so,[4] but in the exercise of the police power it has a very large discretion in that regard—a discretion to which there is no certain and satisfactory limitation,[5] but the power must not be used as a cloak for the invasion of personal rights or private property.[6] In order that a state statute or city ordinance may be sustained as an exercise of the police, the courts must be able to see (1) that the enactment has for its object the prevention of some offence; the preservation of the public health, safety or general welfare;[7] (2) that there is some real and substantial connection between the assumed purpose of the enactment and the actual provision thereto, and that the latter does in some plain, appreciable and appropriate manner tend towards the accomplishment of the object for which the power is used.[8]

Further than this the courts are not concerned regard-

---

[1] Am. and Eng. Ency., Vol. 22, p. 916.
[2] Cooley Const. Line 829.
[3] Lawton vs. State, 152 U. S. 133.
[4] Lawton vs. State, 152 U. S. 133.
[5] Conn. vs. Parks, 155 Mass. 531; People vs. Rosenberg, 128 N. Y. 410.
[6] Lawton vs. Steele, 152 U. S. 133.
[7] State vs. Batement, 10 Ohio, Dec. 68; Lawton vs. Steele, 152 U. S. 133.
[8] Lawton vs. Steele, 152 A. 3, 133.

ing the reasonableness of the exercise of the police power by the legislatures. Thus, the legislature may declare a nuisance and punish individual conduct which is injurious to the health, safety and welfare of the public, though it does not come within the adjudicated scope of the common law offence of a nuisance,[1] and this without violating any constitutional provision, because it makes no compensation to the owner;[2] that is, the legislature does not invade the judicial province by making that unlawful which is not inherently a nuisance.[3]

STATE MAY DELEGATE POWER TO ABATE NUISANCE.— The legislature may, and frequently does, confer upon municipal corporations the power to declare what shall be deemed nuisances within the city limits. A municipal corporation derives its control over nuisances from the legislature creating it. All powers a municipal corporation, created by special or general laws, may exercise, emanate from the state creating it.[4] Therefore, a municipal corporation has only such powers as are expressly delegated to it by the legislature and such implied powers necessary to carry on those expressly granted.

MAY ABATE NUISANCES PER SE WITHOUT GRANT.—It is settled without dissent that, without special grant or authority, municipal corporations may as a common law power cause the abatement of nuisances that are such *per se*.[5] But when city authorities proceed to abate a nuisance, with no authority except that of the common law, they are justified, not because they are officials, but because they are citizens injured by the thing abated,[6] and the extent of municipal authority, as such, over nuisances depends upon powers conferred in this regard upon the municipality. They may be general or specific, or both. The authority to preserve the health and safety of the inhabitants and their property, as well as the authority to prevent and abate nuisances is a sufficient foundation for ordinances to suppress and abate whatever is intrinsically and individually a nuisance.[7]

[1] State vs. McKee, 73 Conn. 18.
[2] Watertown vs. Mayo, 109 U. S. 115.
[3] State vs. Lawer, 185 Mo. 79.
[4] Herman vs. Chicago, 110 Ill. 408.
[5] Rayane vs. Loranger, 66 Mich. 373.
[6] Wood on Nuisances, Sec. 743.
[7] Dillon Municipal Corporations (4th Ed.), Sec. 379.

GENERAL GRANT NOT AUTHORITY TO DECLARE NUIS-
ANCE WHICH IN FACT IS NOT SUCH.—The delegation of
authority over nuisances is very apt to raise troublesome
questions, and the authority itself is likely to be taken as
broader than it is. A municipal corporation, although
authorized in general terms to declare what shall constitute
a nuisance, may not declare that to be a nuisance which in
fact is not.[1] A law that confers upon the common council
"Full power and authority to remove and abate any
nuisance injurious to health or safety" does not confer
upon the council the conclusive jurisdiction to determine
what constitutes a nuisance, but only authorizes the abatement of what is in fact a common nuisance.[2] The United
States Supreme Court, when considering the power conferred upon a city to declare what shall be a nuisance, said,
"It is a doctrine not to be tolerated in this country that
a municipal corporation without express authority from
the legislature, can, by its mere declaration that it is
one, subject it to removal by any person supposed
to be aggrieved, or even by the city itself. This would
place every house, every business, and all the property
of the city at the uncontrolled will of the temporary
authorities."[3]

ORDINANCE MUST BE REASONABLE.—The power to
abate nuisances, like all other municipal powers, must
be reasonably exercised; and, although the power be given
to be exercised in any manner the corporate authorities
may deem expedient, it is not an unlimited power, and
such means only are intended as are reasonably necessary
for the public good. The power to abate nuisances cannot
be so absolute as to be beyond the cognizance of the courts
to determine whether it has been reasonably exercised in
a given case or not.[4] If the power conferred on a municipality is general, then the provision must be reasonable,
and, in fact, it would be poor policy to enact even a valid
ordinance, the enforcement of which would drive away or
annihilate the manufacturing interests of a city. On the
other hand, if, as seems to be true, the emission of dense
smoke may be prevented by the use of mechanical

[1] City of Evansville vs. Miller, 146 Ind. 613; Bank vs. Saralls 129
Ind. 201, and cases cited therein.
[2] Hennessey vs. City of St. Paul.
[3] Yates vs. Milwaukee, 10 Wall U. S. 497.
[4] Rendering Co. vs. Behr, 77 Mo. 91.

devices, or by the employment of competent firemen, or by both, the commercial interests cannot hide behind the expense or the inconvenience of complying with the law.[1] But the power of a court to declare a city ordinance unreasonable, and therefore void, is practically restricted to cases in which the legislature has enacted nothing on the subject matter of the ordinance, or where the same was passed under the supposed incidental power of the corporation merely, or where the municipal corporation has authority only by a general grant.[2]

Where the legislature has given a municipal corporation specific authority to declare under what circumstances the emission of "dense" smoke is a nuisance, and where the municipality has not exceeded the authority granted it, the determination of the city authorities is conclusive of the question.

Much confusion results from the failure to distinguish between the right of a community to abate a public nuisance which is inherent, and in regard to which the important thing is to prove the thing complained of to be a public nuisance, on the one hand, and the purely statutory right of a community to deal with that which the legislature or municipality, properly exercising a delegated police power of the legislature, declares to be a nuisance. One right is a common law right raised by the facts, the other a right lying within the discretion of the legislature, in the exercise of its police power. Smoke alone was not a nuisance at common law, and when a municipality having authority from the legislature only in general terms declares it a nuisance *per se*, that does not make it so, and before it can be held to be a nuisance it must be shown to be an "annoyance and injury to a portion of the inhabitants of the city,"[3] and the difficulty of proving damages in each case practically nullifies a smoke ordinance.

LEGISLATURE MAY CONFER SPECIFIC AUTHORITY.—The legislature may empower the city specifically to declare the emission of dense smoke within the city limits to be a nuisance *per se*, and, having specific authority, it is competent for a municipal corporation to declare that a nuisance which is not so in fact.[4] When the legislature itself

[1] 185 Mo. 79; 16 App. D. C. 428, 29 W. L. B. 364.
[2] A Coal Float vs. City of Jeffersonville, 112 Ind. 15.
[3] St. Louis vs. Packing Co., 141 Mo. 375.
[4] Dillon Minn. Car. Secs., 374, 95.

acts, or authorizes a municipality to act in a definite way and the municipality does so within the authority conferred, the courts will not look too closely at the question of policy or reasonableness.[1] In other words, it is only in extreme cases that the courts have the power to declare a municipal ordinance, passed pursuant to express legislative authority, invalid on the grounds that it is unreasonable, arbitrary and oppressive.[2] What the legislature distinctly says may be done cannot be set aside by the courts because they may deem it unreasonable or against sound policy.[3]

MUST BE CERTAIN, NOT VAGUE IN ITS TERMS.—Granted the proper legislative authority, the power must be exercised by ordinance and not committed to the discretion of municipal officers. A valid ordinance declaring the emission of dense smoke a nuisance, and providing for the abatement of the same, must fix the duty or liability of the citizens by definite, intelligible, prescribed rules, and the rights of a citizen cannot be made to depend on the discretion of any official, high or low.[4]

It had been held by courts that the words "emission of dense black or gray smoke" are vague and uncertain,[5] but these decisions are outweighed by the trend of later decisions throughout the country. It is a practical question, and, as a practical matter, every one knows what is meant by "dense smoke;" it is easily recognized by the sense of sight, and leaves its mark wherever it falls,[6] and it has been demonstrated that convictions may be obtained in the ordinary prosaic manner of asking witnesses of what they have seen. The ordinary man knows what "dense" smoke is and the juryman may be trusted with such testimony. Juries and courts will not pretend to be more ignorant than the rest of mankind.[7] Whether smoke coming fron a chimney or locomotive is "dense" is always a question of fact for the jury.[8]

---

[1] State vs. Favor, 185 Mo. 79; Lawton vs. State, 152 U. S. 133.
[2] 24 Ky. L. Rep. 615.
[3] Dillon Minn. Car. Sec. 328.
[4] St. Louis vs. Packing Co., 14 Mo. 375.
[5] Sigler vs. Cleveland, 3 Nisi Prius.
[6] Harmon vs. Chicago, 110, Ill., 400; St. Paul vs. Hougbro, 100 N. W. 472.
[7] Mum vs. Burch, 25 Ill. 35.
[8] Penn. Co. vs. Chicago, 107, Ill., App. 37.

The exception of private residences from the operations of such ordinances has been often passed upon by the courts, and the law on that may be taken as settled that such exceptions do not invalidate smoke ordinances.[1]

It is further submitted that a municipal corporation, with authority from the legislature by general grant or specific authority to regulate the smoke nuisance, has the power to prevent smoke, by making such provisions for the installation of boilers or the use of mechanical devices, and for proper stoking and firing, as are reasonable.

NOT INTERFERENCE WITH INTERSTATE COMMERCE.— The provision in ordinance to abate smoke as to tugs, locomotives, etc., is upheld on the ground that, while they may engage in interstate commerce and Congress has the power to control interstate commerce, Congress has not yet acted, and it is only repugnant and interfering local legislation that must give way to the paramount laws of Congress constitutionally enacted. Therefore, an ordinance providing for the abatement of dense smoke does not impose any restraint on the use of boats, locomotives, etc., although engaged in general commerce, other than is consistent with law.[2]

LINE OF RECENT DECISIONS.—There is a line of comparatively late decisions that hold smoke ordinances declaring the emission of "dense" smoke to be a nuisance *per se*, and passed pursuant to a general grant of power from the legislature, valid. A typical and much-quoted case on both points, viz., the delegation of police power to a municipal corporation and that smoke is a nuisance *per se*, is Harmon vs. Chicago (110 Ill. 400). After a close reading of the case, one can only conjecture whether the court would have upheld the ordinance had it not so definitely made up its mind that "dense" smoke is a nuisance *per se* in populous cities. Holding "dense" smoke in a populous city a nuisance *per se* enabled the court to bridge over some troublesome questions as to the authority of a municipal corporation to deal with what it had declared to be a nuisance. This case is valuable because it expresses the healthy doctrine that the emission of "dense" smoke in populous cities is a nuisance in itself, enabling municipal corporations to abate "dense" smoke without specific authority from the legislature.

[1] 86 Mich. 273; 110, Ill., 400; 85 Mo. 79.
[2] Harmon vs. Chicago, 110, Ill., 400.

Courts do not require proof that fire will burn, or that powder will explode, or that many other processes of nature and art produce certain known effects.[1] So courts have taken judicial notice of the fact known to all men that the emission and discharge of dense smoke into the atmosphere in a large and populous city is of itself a nuisance to the general public of such city; is injurious to vegetation, to many kinds of goods, and annoying to the people. This knowledge is so generally diffused in large cities that no court or jury could be without it.[2] In other words, in these decisions, courts hold that which was not a nuisance *per se* at common law, may be such in a populous city, and thereby confer upon municipal corporations ample power to effectually deal with, prevent and abate a nuisance which of recent years has greatly interfered with the health, comfort and convenience of those who congregate in great centers of population and which arises from the complex conditions of modern life. Such decisions are in line with the enlightened judicial opinions which recognize the plenary power of a municipality to deal with, prevent and abate those things which result in annoyance, inconvenience and discomfiture, as nuisances which were not recognized as such under the general principle of the common law, but in recent years have come to be such in many of our large cities. At common law a nuisance was anything that worked hurt, inconvenience or damage. A common or public nuisance was that which affected the public, or was an annoyance to the king's subjects at large. Precisely, that is the character of "dense" smoke.[3] The decisions that recognize "dense" smoke in a populous city as a nuisance *per se*, conform to the idea that the law is a progressive science, and have been valuable in several cities in preventing and abating the emission of smoke.

In conclusion, we may say that the source of authority to prevent and abate the smoke nuisance is the police power of the state; the state may delegate this authority to municipal corporations; at common law "dense" smoke was not a nuisance *per se*, and is not such now in most jurisdictions, except in those jurisdictions where courts

[1] State vs. Hayes, 78 Mo. 307–318.
[2] Field & Co. vs. Chicago, 44 Ill. App. 410.
[3] Harmon vs. Chicago, 110, Ill., 400.

have held "dense" smoke in a populous city to be a nuisance *per se*, and, to deal with as such, must have specific authority from the legislature; the power must be exercised by statute or ordinance, which must be definite, intelligible and reasonable, and must not again be delegated to municipal officers, high, or low, in their discretion either to declare or define; where the right created by the legislature arises under a general power and not by specific authority to declare and abate "dense" smoke a nuisance *per se*, it is the duty of the court in every case upon proper proof to decide whether the facts constitute a nuisance; and where the right created by the legislature arises under specific authority to declare "dense" smoke a nuisance, it is the duty of the court to decide whether the facts constitute what the legislature or the common council, assuming a proper exercise of the power granted it, had declared and defined as a nuisance.

In view of the advanced legislation and judicial decisions in recent years, we may well say that the law pertaining to the smoke nuisance is progressive, and will keep pace with the popular sentiment regarding the emission of "dense" smoke into the air in large centers of population.

5. RAILROAD SMOKE

THE SMOKE NUISANCE ON LOCOMOTIVES *

By GEORGE W. WELDEN, Superintendent of Motive Power on the
New York, New Haven & Hartford Railroad

We appreciate your kind invitation, granting us the privilege of having a representative here to say something on the subject in question, and to explain as best we can our attitude, efforts and desires in connection with the matter of smoke abatement or elimination.

In the remarks that follow, what I shall say regarding conditions on the New York, New Haven & Hartford Railroad will, I think, apply generally to all railroads using bituminous coal as a fuel on locomotives and is, therefore, not a local problem, although I may deal with it in more or less of a personal manner in my references.

As operating officials, our interest in this subject is two-fold. First, we recognize the inconveniences and discomforts such a nuisance causes our patrons traveling on our trains as well as that portion of the public who are so unfortunate (in this respect) as to dwell along our line, and second, because of the enormous economy and saving to be effected in favor of the railroad company could the desired results in smoke consumption be fully accomplished.

As I was looking over an advance copy of your program, which your secretary kindly sent me, I came across the following lines which were inserted as a sort of introductory to the importance of the subject. They run as follows: "No comment is needed as to the importance of dealing with the smoke nuisance. Everywhere in our large cities it is only too prominent and too much in evidence. How to abate it is a difficult question." To my mind, no lines could be penned that would more exactly express the real conditions, both as to the importance of the subject and the difficulty in dealing with it, than those just quoted.

As a general proposition, railroad companies are assumed, by the rank and file, to take only such interest in the question of smoke elimination on locomotives as they are actually compelled to through the clamor of the public and the penalties imposed or prescribed by ordinances and enforced by the courts. If the above assumption were really true, then rail-

*Read at the Providence Meeting of the American Civic Association, November 20, 1907.

road operation in general could be properly classed as the most miserably managed business in the world. The New York, New Haven & Hartford Railroad, while constituting but a small percentage of the railroad mileage of the United States, and necessarily consuming but a small proportion of the total fuel burned on all railroads, could save annually for its treasury approximately $600,000 if some good Samaritan would suggest a method or device by means of which the black smoke and unconsumed gases which now escape from the smoke stacks of our locomotives could be completely burned and used as effective fuel. Second to the above-mentioned saving would be that accruing to the treasury because of the absence of the necessity of defending damage cases before the courts, involving, as they do, hundreds of thousands of dollars, and, naturally, the saving of the very large sums paid annually in fines. In addition to this, many incidental savings would be made in the form of less labor and time required to clean all classes of equipment both inside and out, including an increased life for the varnish on all classes of equipment. Coupled with this would be a decidedly improved appearance.

What has been said should suffice to impress you with the idea that we at least realize in the keenest sense our situation and what great economies there are ahead if we can only reach them. You may also have gathered the impression that we consider the abatement of the smoke nuisance on locomotives a hopeless task and, as a matter of fact, are ready to throw up our hands. To this I desire to say that we are still optimists on the subject. We still have hopes.

I presume it will be of interest to you to know what has really been done in the past in the way of fighting this monster, what is being done at present, and also the future outlook.

In the past we have tried not only on our locomotives, but also on our stationary plants, every known device and method brought to our attention which, in our mechanical judgment, had the least semblance of a promise of success, and this, too, without regard to the first cost of application, which, in many cases, amounted to a considerable sum. Up to, but not including, our present experiments, we have, without exception, met only with signal defeat.

The primary cause of my appearing before you today in the rôle of a smoke champion is not because of my fame as an expert on this subject, but principally because your President reads the papers and had noticed an account in one of the scientific periodicals explaining at great length and with considerable color the great success the New Haven Road was having with a new type of smoke consumer then being tried on one of their locomotives. He desired that the details and workings of this device and its success be brought to your attention.

As the New Haven Road is at present experimenting or arranging to experiment with four different patented devices for consuming the smoke on locomotives, and as we must, as a matter of fairness and policy, refrain from advocating in advance any particular device, it is not therefore within my province either to minutely describe or express a preference for one as against the other. We hope they will all do well.

The particular device described in the newspaper article referred to and the one that has been the longest on trial did have at first great promise of success, and we sincerely hoped to have something really good to offer this Association at this meeting on a subject on which they are so deeply interested; but we have met with so many obstacles in the course of operation that we do not feel like raising your hopes too high, and will only say now that we feel that in time we may be able to overcome some of these and yet realize the promised success, as we feel there is still considerable merit in the device. We have enough confidence in its merits at least to begin at the first and do our work all over again. I will hazard this opinion on the device: If we can manage to keep the mechanism together and make the device commercially practicable, it would almost completely consume the smoke, I might say would rival hard-coal-burning locomotives. Other similar devices now under test are practically in the same degree of perfection and are as yet only experiments.

Considering the present development of the art of smoke consumption on locomotives with the incomplete devices so far produced for eliminating the smoke, there seems, at present, but one alternative left, and one through which immediate relief may be had; and that is the good intelligent fireman, the only real smoke-preventer just now. It is to this individual that we have turned our undivided attention and are making every effort to instruct him and educate him as fully as possible how to fire a locomotive so as to get both economy in fuel and at the same time prevent making great clouds of dense, black smoke. To the uninitiated this matter of educating engineers and firemen with reference to smoke prevention might seem an easy or insignificant matter, but you will more fully realize what a great task it is and why better results are not had in general throughout the country when you understand that on the New York, New Haven & Hartford Railroad alone there are one thousand five hundred locomotive engineers, each an individual handling his locomotive in his own peculiar way, and yet conforming, in this respect, to what is usually termed good practice. With these one thousand five hundred engineers are one thousand five hundred firemen, upon whose skill in handling the scoop depends the degree in which the black smoke nuisance is eliminated. If these firemen were a fixture, as it were, the training feature of the work would not be so great, but they are constantly going and coming all the time, making it necessary to keep continually posting new men as to their duties. Some idea of the difficulties we experience in this direction may be gathered from the fact that during the year just passed we have taken into our service as firemen on locomotives one thousand green men, or about 66 per cent of the total force of firemen has been renewed in order to keep the quota complete. Can we really wonder then that the results are not what they should be?

The smoke nuisance on locomotives stands then in about the light in which I have described it, and I can assure you that it will certainly be as great or greater relief to the railroad companies as to the public in general, when some real inventive genius comes to the front with a practical smoke consumer, one which will operate and do its work as successfully as other parts of the locomotive are now doing. The New Haven Road stands ready to try, and will welcome any device or method that has promise of success. The cost of application need not cause very great concern, if the device or method is fully demonstrated to be a success in every particular.

THE RAILWAY SMOKE PROBLEM

By A. W. GIBBS, General Superintendent of Motive Power, Pennsylvania Railroad*

Your Secretary has very courteously requested that we prepare for the Annual Meeting of the Association a statement showing what progress the Pennsylvania Railroad Company is making in the suppression of smoke nuisance from locomotives, and in the following paper we will endeavor to show: (*a*) What has been accomplished; (*b*) What we may hope to accomplish; and, (*c*) The reasons why more has not been accomplished.

*Read at the Pittsburgh Meeting of the American Civic Association, November 19, 1908.

To clearly state the case, we think some fundamental facts should be agreed upon.

Comparisons are continually being made between the railroads of this country and those of foreign lands, and these comparisons, while admitting certain great accomplishments performed by our roads, also dwell on our shortcomings, and in no direction more vigorously than as regards the emission of smoke, and the query which continually arises is: Why, when the railroads have accomplished so much in other directions, have we today an equal or greater amount of smoke than we had many years ago? Is it because the railroads are supine in this matter? Or, is it because the problem is one not capable of solution?

The railroads are not supine in this matter. They are officered and manned by good citizens, whose interest is really that of the rest of the community; usually, they live along the line of the road with which they are connected; the smoke that annoys others vexes them to an equal or greater extent; and, aside from their duty as citizens, is the strong motive of self-interest to escape annoyance for reasons of personal comfort.

OWNERSHIP.—Ignoring, for the present, any difference which naturally exists in the fuels used, it should be remembered that on some roads, particularly those of the continent, state ownership is quite general, and such roads have behind them the financial, as well as the moral, backing of the states. Each road is not obligated to the same extent to pay its way, the comparison being somewhat like that of the Postal Service of our government; for, if the revenue of the Postal Department is not equal to the expenditures, a Deficiency Bill remedies the difficulty.

Again, the government has power in the direction of enforcing discipline, not delegated to private owners; but on this phase of the question more will be said later.

In our land, the railroads, to a great extent, have grown up with the country; in fact, in the greater part of it, it may be said that the railroad came first and the population afterwards. While public ownership has been tried in various states, it has never been associated, so far as we are aware, with good or successful management, and it was long ago recognized that the burden of the development of railroad transportation in this country should be settled by private ownership, rather than by that of the state or national government, and thus, although such states as Pennsylvania, Virginia, North Carolina, Georgia, and probably others, at one time owned or operated railroads, at the present time no state is engaged in the operation of any railroad, and state ownership of securities of railroads within their borders has largely disappeared.

The development of the country thus devolved on chartered companies, which had to secure the necessary funds from public subscription. With the risks that attended such investment of capital, it became essential that these roads must be able to manufacture and sell transportation at a profit, having no revenue—if we neglect the Land-Grant roads—other than the sale 'of transportation. To induce the investment of money of the public, returns in the form of dividends must be made; otherwise, capital will seek other outlet and the development of the roads will cease. More than this, the road which cannot manufacture its transportation for less than it sells it will inevitably go through the bankruptcy court.

Costs Must Be Considered.—Today, the railroads are facing the problem of increased costs of all factors which go to make the cost of transportation, whether it be material purchased, labor required, additional taxes, etc., and this with Governmental restrictions in the selling price of the product. It must be clear, therefore, that, with the duty of affording to the public thoroughly good service, the question of costs cannot be overlooked.

Some Governing Factors.—With the railroads of this country, the prime essential in manufacturing cheap transportation is the possibility of hauling large train units. In this we differ radically from the railroads of other countries with which comparisons are most frequently made; that is to say, more frequent and lighter units are the rule. This means that in this country the locomotive has developed into a power plant of the most concentrated character. For instance, where with a stationary plant we are satisfied to burn from 15 to 20 pounds of coal per square foot of grate surface, per hour, in many of our locomotives we must be able to burn not less than 100 pounds of coal per square foot of grate surface within the same period of time. In a stationary plant, fluctuations in the demand are comparatively slight, and can usually be anticipated and prepared for in advance, while with the locomotive, on the other hand, we must be able to vary the output enormously within an extremely short period of time. For instance, a locomotive may be working at full power, producing little smoke, and be suddenly forced to shut off or stop, under which condition the fire will not adapt itself immediately to the changed requirements, and, even with care, under such circumstances, the emission of smoke is certain. The reason for this is that, while working with forced draft, there is a fair balance between the rate at which the coal is consumed and the air drawn over the fire to complete the combustion, and the volatile material is distilling off at a fairly uniform rate. With the cessation of the draft, but with the coal still emitting quantities of volatile gases, air is not drawn in in sufficient quantity, with the result so frequently experienced. Again, many coals which, when burned in a leisurely manner, give little or no visible smoke, will give great annoyance when the rate of combustion is doubled or trebled as the case may be. Consequently, it may reasonably be expected that terminals in level country, where trains can be handled in and out of the station without excessive demand on the locomotive, are likely to be more nearly smokeless than those where the locomotive must be overworked from the start.

LIMITATIONS OF SIZE.—Limitations of space, such as width of gauge, tunnels, bridges and other clearances, restrict us in the possible dimensions of the locomotive power plant; consequently, the whole plant—particularly the boiler—is operated at an intensity nowhere else required. This is the crux of the whole situation; for while it is possible to burn almost any fuel smokelessly, provided the operation be not too hurried, it requires considerable skill and the best appliances to do so when the rate of combustion is forced to the utmost.

The question may now very properly be asked: How do the conditions of the present day differ from those of the past, and why is this question of smoke prevention more important now than ever before?

In answer to this it may be stated: First, that while the design of the locomotive in its essential details differs but slightly from the older types, there has been a great increase in the number and size of the locomotives and in the demands made on them. Secondly, it is to be noted that the complaint against smoke usually comes from cities and towns, rather than from the country. This is natural, for the reason that there are more people and more locomotives at the terminal, and it is just there that conditions are naturally the worst, for it is at the terminals where old fires must be cleaned and new ones started. It is then, of all times, that smoke is most unavoidable. It is also true that many railroads have built their terminals in what was then the country, but cities have grown up around them, and with the growth come the complaints. The public demands facilities in the heart of business centers, in order to cheapen drayage and afford convenient access for travelers.

OTHER SOURCES OF SMOKE.—Again, it must be borne in mind that the railroads are not the only factors in the problem. In any city where bituminous coal is used for domestic fires and for stationary plants, the increase in the amount of smoke made over previous years is almost directly proportional to the increase in population and manufacturing industries; and while many of the manufacturing plants have made great progress in the reduction of smoke, the restrictions brought about by municipal agitation have been the cause, in more than one case, of the removal to other locations.

In the case of the domestic fire, little or no progress has been made, from the standpoint of reduction in the amount and character of the smoke, nor is improvement probable, on account of conditions. While one of these little chimneys may not attract much attention from the smoke which it emits, they are responsible, in the aggregate, for a very great part of the total defilement. It has been proved that the combustion in the domestic fire is apt to be far less complete than in the case of industrial or locomotive fires, for the reason that the consumption is usually very sluggish and a considerable amount of tarry matter exudes and is carried off as soot, whereas in the other fire the temperature is high enough to insure relatively complete combustion. Many municipal ordinances establishing penalties for the emission of black smoke expressly exempt the domestic chimney, and wisely so, for the reason that no remedy for this condition of smokiness has been presented, and many householders cannot afford to purchase the high-priced smokeless fuels; but this much should be clearly understood, that the domestic fire largely influences the general condition, due to the great number of small contributions, and for the same reason it should be understood that every encouragement should be offered the housekeeper to use a smokeless fuel, if possible.

METHODS OF SOLVING PROBLEM.—With the foregoing difficulties set forth, the citizen will naturally ask of the railroad: What have you done, and what are you going to do?

The means which the railroad has at its command for the elimination of smoke, are: (1) The use of comparatively smokeless fuels; (2) The use of devices of various kinds which may allow the use of otherwise smoky fuels; and, (3) Education of the men operating locomotives and supervising their work.

FUEL AVAILABLE.—It is evident that the railroads must produce power with the fuel of the country through which they run, and a glance at a geological map of this country will convince any one that bituminous coal is that with which this question must be settled. Of the other fuels, anthracite is confined to practically a few counties in the eastern part of Pennsylvania. The amount of anthracite mined is a trifle more than 70,000,000 tons each year. It is the ideal fuel for domestic purposes and for use in plants where its cost is not prohibitive. The total amount is so limited, however, that, were the demand to be on this fuel alone, the supply would be inadequate, in illustration of which, we submit the following statement of the consumption, for the fiscal year ending June 30, 1907, on twenty railroads which, from their geographical location, would naturally have the first claims on this fuel, for the reason that they are nearest the anthracite field, viz:

	Anthracite Coal (Tons)	Bituminous Coal (Tons)
Pennsylvania Railroad Company	61,297.25	7,159,627.55
Pennsylvania Company		2,128,994.00
Northern Central Railway Company....	22,364.00	604,856.00
Phila., Baltimore & Washington R. R. ...		637,765.45
Long Island Railroad	156,494.84	155,618.52
Pgh., Cincinnati, Chicago & St. Louis Ry.		1,758,501.00
Vandalia Railroad		560,973.00
Grand Rapids & Indiana Railroad......		214,461.00
Baltimore & Ohio Railroad	20,451.05	4,782,434.25
New York Central & Hudson River R. R.	216,624.00	4,242,476.00
Michigan Central Railroad		1,245,628.00
Lake Shore and Michigan Southern Ry..		1,998,902.00
Lake Erie & Western Railroad		300,613.00
New York, Chicago & St. Louis Railroad		539,614.00
Central Railroad of New Jersey	607,617.00	318,348.50
Delaware & Hudson Company	902,769.00	196,183.00
New York, New Haven & Hartford R.R.	34,268.00	1,830,701.00
Boston & Maine Railroad		1,440,454.00
Erie Railroad	263,158.00	2,216,058.00
Philadelphia & Reading Railway	1,145,134.70	903,565.10

These roads consume annually some thirty-five and two-third million tons, three and one-half million tons of which is anthracite. Assuming that the entire consumption of these roads were anthracite, it will be seen that this small group alone would consume more than one-half of the total amount of anthracite mined. While such action would doubtless stimulate the production, it would but hasten the disappearance of this most valuable fuel, to say nothing of the enhancement in price which would most assuredly follow and directly affect every householder now dependent on this fuel. Granting that the anthracite thus absorbed by the railroads were replaced by bituminous coal for domestic purposes, the smoke situation would be far worse than at the present because the numerous small domestic fires, with the usually imperfect combustion, produce more total smoke than would the same amount of bituminous coal burned in locomotive furnaces. The item of cost to the railroads would be such a tremendous increase in their expenses as to make it absolutely prohibitive. A recent study of this subject showed that on nineteen of the principal roads, the fuel bill exceeded 11.4 per cent of the total operating expense, or nearly 8 per cent of the gross earnings.

Coke.—The total production of coke is about thirty-six million tons annually, which is almost entirely used in metallurgical work, for which there is no substitute. Remembering that in the production of coke from bituminous coal there is an initial waste of about one-third of the heating value of the fuel, with further losses from breakage in handling, it is evident that this attempted solution would be an unpardonable waste of our natural resources.

However, in the endeavor to obviate smoke, a great many attempts have been made to use coke, and the records of the tests show that the results have been very unsatisfactory, owing to the difficulty with which the fuel is handled,—at times the heat being entirely too intense and at others the fire being almost stopped up by the ashes produced. It must not be forgotten that in the process of burning coal to coke the ash originally in the coal remains in the coke, so that in burning a ton of coke much more ash results than from the consumption of a ton of the coal from which it was made. The coke, when used, is satisfactory in but one particular, namely, its freedom from smoke.

The reason that anthracite and coke are smokeless, is because of the large percentage of fixed carbon and the small percentage of volatile or flame- and smoke-producing material; for instance, the fixed carbon may run as high as 90 per cent, volatile matter not over 4 per cent; the remainder being ash and sulphur.

BITUMINOUS COAL.—Of bituminous coal, somewhat over 400,000,000 tons are mined annually, and the total consumption of this fuel by the railroads of this country is estimated to closely approximate 100,000,000 tons. This railroad consumption, it will be noticed, is almost sufficient to exhaust the present total production of both anthracite and coke, so that we may as well admit that, this being a bituminous coal country, it is this fuel alone that we must consider in solving this smoke problem; although possibly in certain restricted localities we may be justified on entirely disregarding all questions of expense and using only smokeless fuel—this for the sole purpose of controlling the smoke.

CHEMISTRY OF BITUMINOUS COALS.—The composition of our various bituminous coals differs widely. Some of them are relatively smokeless. Chemically, these are characterized by the great amount of fixed carbon and the small amount of volatile or flame- and smoke-producing constituents. Approximately, these may range from 70 to 80 per cent fixed carbon, from 15 to 22 per cent volatile matter, the remainder being moisture, ash and sulphur. On the other hand, some of the highly bituminous coals will contain less than 50 per cent fixed carbon, and over 40 per cent volatile material, and it is with such wide variations in composition that the question must be settled.

It is customary to group under the head of "volatile material" all the substances which will distill from the coal when heated in a closed tube; but, on examination, it is found that the composition of this material is quite complex, and it does not follow at all that the volatile material of one coal differs only in amount from that of another grade. While much has yet to be learned of the ultimate composition of this material, it is safe to say that some contain more of the smoke- or soot-producing constituents than others. In other words, some bituminous coals, while containing approximately the same percentage of volatile material, are more difficult to burn without the emission of smoke.

The low-volatile bituminous coals have, unfortunately, the peculiarity that they are extremely friable and, even though mined in lumpy form, will very speedily break up into small size; and although this does not interfere with their usefulness where burned slowly, it is a very serious hindrance to their use in locomotive boilers when worked to the fullest capacity, for the reason that the powerful draft throws out of the chimney a very large part of the fuel put into the firebox, and, while at low rates of combustion this is the most efficient of our bituminous coals, this condition does not hold true when the demands on the locomotive are increased. For locomotive purposes, the physical structure of the coal is actually more important than the chemical composition. The important requirements are that the coal shall be fairly lumpy; that it shall be fairly uniform in size; that it shall not readily break up in the atmosphere; and that it shall retain its form in the firebox. When these conditions are met, such fuel can be burned with comparatively little smoke, owing to the possibility of maintaining a thin, bright fire.

BRIQUETTES.—A possibility of the future, not yet fully developed, is the use of smokeless or low-volatile coals made into briquettes by the addition of suitable binding material, after which the fuel is pressed into large blocks. This practice, long known and utilized abroad, is now being developed in this country, very intelligent work being done by the United States Geological Survey, and, while at present the cost of fuel so produced is so high as to be prohibitive, it is hoped that this method of preparing fuel may ultimately prove a factor in relieving the smoke nuisance.

OIL FUEL.—Oil fuel is largely used in some parts of the Southwest, where there are great deposits of oil, otherwise of little value. Owing to the distance and the difficulties of transportation, it is not likely that this fuel can be considered as one available for railroads other than those in the territory where such oil abounds, and it may be dimissed from our consideration.

To recapitulate: Anthracite, coke and low-volatile bituminous coal are all being used, to greater or lesser extent, at various points where the smoke condition is most pronounced, in order to minimize the annoyance; but, as has been pointed out, the extension of the use of such fuels is distinctly limited, and the great questiom remains:

By what appliances or methods, without annoyance to the community, shall we successfully burn the bituminous coal which must be our reliance?

REQUIREMENTS FOR SMOKELESS COMBUSTION.—There is probably no railroad of importance which has not from time to time introduced appliances for this purpose. The basis on which the devices are planned is as follows: (1) To distil the volatile gases at as uniform a rate as possible. (2) To present to the burning gases an adequate supply of air to effect complete combustion. (3) To thoroughly mix this air with the gases. (4) To effect this mixture while the gases are still at a very high temperature. (5) To allow sufficient time for this mixture and combustion of the air and gases to take place before the heat is absorbed and the temperature reduced below the combustion point. With these five conditions complied with, the whole difficulty is overcome, and just in so far as the devices meet these five conditions are they successful.

DEVICES.—A bare mention of all these devices would be tedious, but it may not be amiss to indicate some of the methods by which this has been attempted.

The first condition is the manual one of introducing the coal steadily and in small quantities, preferably allowing it to coke near the door.

The brick arch placed across the lower forward end of the firebox and inclined upward and toward the rear acts as a baffle to increase the distance that the burning gases must flow before the cooling of the flame is effected. In this process, the arch becomes intensely hot, thus maintaining the high temperature while the fire-door is momentarily opened. This device partly meets conditions 4 and 5 and, when supplemented by judicious air admission above the fire, partly meets the last four conditions. This —one of the oldest devices—is possibly the best, and was once the general standard for locomotives of the Pennsylvania and other railroads. The reason why it was not maintained is that its presence in the firebox is a very serious obstacle to the proper and frequent inspection of the interior, on the perfection of which examination safety hinges. The arch remains incandescent for a long period, thus making proper inspection impracticable. The other reason for its disuse is that the locomotive is a power plant of such concentrated character and so highly forced that the arch alone, without very intelligent firing, will not prevent smoke. To illustrate, it is perfectly practicable to operate at moderate power with such an absence of smoke that for periods of more than one-half hour not a particle of smoke will be visible; but let the conditions change, now shutting off, now working to the utmost limit of capacity, and smoke at once appears, because the device will not adapt itself to these extreme conditions.

Other devices embody one or more of the following: Air-pipes through the sides of the firebox to admit air to meet conditions 2 and 3; this is only partially effective. Again, air-pipes more or less exposed to the heat of the fire so as to preheat the air, are tried, thus attempting to meet conditions 2, 3 and 4. The difficulty with this type is that the heat of the fire usually destroys the device. Still others employ steam jets, sometimes superheated, to thoroughly mix the gases and comply with conditions 2 and 3. Then there is the constantly recurring attempt to bring back to the firebox some of the smokebox gases, as well as the partly burned cinders there collected. This has never been developed to an extent to afford any promise.

AUTOMATIC STOKERS.—In this connection, while considering devices, we cannot omit all reference to the question of automatic stokers. The general progress demands transferring the burden of great manual exertion from the man to a machine, the latter doing the hard work and the man supervising the action of the machine. With this end in view, a great deal has been and is being done in the direction of developing automatic stokers which will do the firing with a certain amount of manual supervision. Of these devices, quite a number have been devised and put into use on locomotives. So far, they have not proven satisfactory and, from their imperfections, have not improved the smoke conditions, but the demand for them is so urgently recognized by the railroads, not only from the mere smoke question, but also on account of the saving in money and relief to labor, that there is ground for hope that in the comparatively near future, a satisfactory automatic stoker will be developed. The problem is a most difficult one, and notwithstanding the fact that the brightest and most practical minds are hard at work on a solution, it is difficult to predict when success will be reached.

The automatic stoker, when perfected, promises to be one of the most effective appliances to aid in the suppression of smoke, for the reason that it does not become tired from the hard work and, consequently, should do as well after hours of service as in the beginning. The contrary is the case with the man. For this reason, the stoker, when perfected, will come to stay.

The gist of the matter is that devices alone, unless supplemented by intelligent and unremitting attention, never long survive. They start with a blare of trumpets; they show a decided improvement over previous conditions; then less is heard of them; and, finally, when inquiry is made, it is found that they have been removed as inefficient. The real reason is that while new they receive a degree of attention that makes them more or less successful, and the credit is ascribed largely to the device, when it is actually due to the care.

Evidently, the real line of progress is to stimulate and maintain the intelligent care, and it is in the latter direction that the most progress is being made, and where there is the greatest hope for the future.

SUPERVISION.—Let us now consider what we believe to be the ultimate solution of the problem, without which the best fuel, and the best appliances, will not be effective in reducing smoke, namely, the education and supervision of the men running and firing locomotives.

It must be remembered that on a large railroad system there are thousands of men firing and handling locomotives. First, we have the engineman, who runs the machine and upon whose careful and judicious handling the ease of proper firing largely depends; secondly, we have the fireman, whose skill and interest in properly firing the locomotive must never flag for an instant; third, we have engine-preparers and ashpitmen at engine-houses, who must understand how to clean old fires and build new ones with a minimum amount of smoke.

With the rapid growth of business and consequent increase in the number of employes, it must be realized that supervision in this sense requires a large force of men, for the reason that, owing to the extent of the territory over which any group of locomotives and men run, following up any particular set of men is a very different proposition from that of supervising a very much greater number of men grouped in some one place, as, for instance, in a large power-house.

The supervision, to be effective, involves, first, accurate

instruction, and, secondly, repeated personal visitation to see whether this is followed, and, third, discipline if the instruction is persistently disregarded, either from inability or indifference, and the correction of abuses, such as the improper preparation of the locomotive for the run.

To show how this supervision is being effected, it must be understood that the organization of the railroad is practically a military one. On each division, the man in charge of the enginemen and firemen, under the Superintendent, is the Road Foreman of Engines, who has assistants, each in charge of districts containing a certain number of locomotives and men. In some cases it is the practice for these assistants to have subordinates to instruct in firing, although the tendency is to put in this position men taken from the ranks of the enginemen, so that their rank will carry authority to instruct both enginemen and firemen. In addition, smoke inspectors, whose entire duty is to report locomotives emitting black smoke, are stationed at various points along the division.

PRINTED INSTRUCTIONS.—The management has prepared definite and uniform instructions, in printed form, which have been placed in the hands of all men responsible for operating, firing and attending to locomotives on the road and at terminals. From these instructions we quote the following, which pertain particularly to the elimination of smoke, namely:

"Enginemen and firemen must work together so as to save coal and reduce smoke."

"The burning of bituminous coal in a locomotive requires air, which must be admitted through the grates and through the fire-door."

"Smoke means waste of coal and must be avoided."

"Large quantities of coal placed in the firebox at one time cool down the fire, cause smoke and waste coal; small quantities at regular intervals will keep the fire bright, prevent smoke and take less coal to keep up steam pressure."

"Lumps of coal should be broken in pieces not larger than three inches."

"A bright and level fire over the whole grate must be carried wherever possible. When a sloping fire is used, no more coal should be banked at the door than is necessary."

"To prevent smoke and to save coal, the fire-door must be placed on or against the latch after firing coal or using the scraper, slash-bar or hook, and when on siding, in yards, at terminals, or before starting."

"Before the throttle is closed, the blower must be used and the door placed on the latch. Firemen must stop firing long enough before steam is shut off to prevent smoke and waste of coal."

Under present-day conditions, more supervision is required than formerly, on account of the rapid increase in railway business, necessitating the employment and the promotion of men who have not been through the long course of probation formerly the rule. Furthermore, the importance of educating and developing intelligent supervising officers in order to reach the men, is of late being recognized. At Altoona, there has been installed a testing plant consisting of a locomotive whose driving wheels rest on suitable supporting wheels placed underneath and taking the place of the usual track, the whole locomotive being firmly connected to a dynamometer that maintains it in position while recording the work performed by the locomotive, so that it is operated in the usual way and produces the usual pull. It is otherwise stationary, subject to careful inspection and test entirely impracticable with the same locomotive running free on the road. By means of this plant, which is entirely devoted to the purpose of securing information, we are educating our officers interested in the fuel question to its possibilities, so that they may thoroughly understand how to instruct the men to carry out the definite printed instructions.

Furthermore, we are recognizing the necessity for greater supervision by the appointment of a greater number of supervising officers, so that the number of men under the jurisdiction of each will be small enough to admit of constant personal contact.

It must not be forgotten in this connection that the cost of the supervision mentioned in the foregoing is a very serious burden on the cost of operation, and while the railroads would not provide such supervision but for the belief that it will yield adequate return, or, from realization of the duties which the railroads owe the public, there must be a limit to the amount of money which the railroads can so expend.

As stated before, the cost of fuel is from 8 to 11 per cent

of the total operating cost of a railroad, and, therefore, ecomomy in the consumption of fuel is one of the most obvious ways of reducing operating expenses. Fortunately, the methods described in the foregoing for the elimination of smoke from locomotives are also those which must be followed in order to obtain the maximum economy in locomotive fuel consumption; in other words, the crew making the least smoke saves the most coal. It follows, therefore, that the railroads have a direct financial interest in the elimination of smoke to the lowest possible limit.

It will be noted that, so far, nothing has been said of the possible solution by electrification.

This Company, as you know, is now engaged in the development of terminals in the neighborhood of New York City, where electric traction is the only thing to be considered, owing to the use of deep sub-aqueous tunnels. This Company is also operating, in the state of New Jersey, a fairly long line on which multiple-unit electric trains are operated. While avoiding technicalities, we will briefly state that the multiple-unit system of electric traction consists of nothing more than an electric road on which either single cars or sections of two or more cars —each car having its separate motor and control apparatus—are formed in trains, all the motors being operated by one motorman. This form of transit is doubtless familiar to all of you, and is feasible on the road in question in so far as passenger movement is concerned, because it is, in a measure, an isolated road and does not have to face many of the long-distance problems; but the freight business has to be handled by steam locomotives.

In the New York installation, we are confronted by the problem of both multiple-unit trains and of through trains hauled by electric locomotives. It is but fair to say that while the multiple-unit train seems to be fairly well worked out, the problem of the electric locomotive is far from a satisfactory solution and, although unremitting attention has been given to the subject for years past, it still remains in the experimental stage.

In the same locality,—namely on the New York Central and the New York, New Haven & Hartford Railroads,— are two other systems of electric traction. In the former, electric current is transmitted to the train by means of contact of a sliding shoe with a third-rail placed at the side of the running track, while on the New York, New Haven & Hartford Railroad, the transmission is from a suitably supported trolley wire placed above the tracks. Both methods have serious objections, but the question of an electric locomotive of adequate power and of thoroughly good stability for running has yet to be developed.

The cost of everything electric is tremendous. The electric locomotives, such as they are, cost more than double the steam locomotives that they replace, and with this but a small part of the story has been told, as we must add the cost of track preparation, of the power plants and all that goes to make the electric system as a whole.

The demand has frequently been made that if not the entire cross-country line, the cities or terminals should be electrified. In some cases, the same demand has been made where cities are not terminals for any but a small proportion of the trains running into them, which would mean, for a city where this practice might prevail, two locomotive terminals, one on each side of the city, electrification of the space within the city limits, with a supply of special electric locomotives, and the delay of a double stop, to say nothing of the difficulties due to the interruptions of such functions as the steam heating of trains. To offset the cost of this, there is no saving whatever in operation; on the contrary, the operating cost is largely increased. If the railroads could stand the burden of cost, it is certain that the public itself would not tolerate unnecessary delays of this kind.

While anything of the kind is possible from an unlimited expenditure of money, we do not hesitate to say that the time has not yet come when the enormous outlay of capital for the purpose of electrification of the railroads would be justified by the returns, and, further, we assert that the capital thus diverted would be far more useful in other directions.

LARGE SAVING BY CAREFUL STOKING

Mr. Angus Sinclair, President of the Society of Locomotive Engineers, in his book on locomotive-firing, pages 26 and 27, gives his experience with two firemen on the same locomotive, running the same distance, on two successive days. The first fireman, in one hour and fifty-five minutes, the time occupied in the run, used eight thousand pounds of soft coal, making steam with difficulty, and filling the atmosphere with smoke. The next day, another fireman, with the same engine, running the same distance, used forty-five hundred pounds of the same coal, with plenty of steam and no smoke. The result was a saving of 43¾ per cent of coal, and no annoyance from smoke. As the first condition is pretty nearly universal on roads where soft coal is used, the loss to the roads from ignorance or carelessness must be enormous.

BALTIMORE & OHIO RAILROAD

As a general rule, we believe we can successfully fire our engines with soft, bituminous coal, which is mined on the line of the Baltimore & Ohio, and which, with scientific firing, can be burned without the emission of black smoke.

I. H. MUHFELD, General Superintendent of Motive Power.

MEXICAN CENTRAL RAILROAD

The Mexican Central Railroad is buying from the Mexican Petroleum Company 4,000 barrels of fuel oil daily, at a cost of $1.10 per barrel. The road is increasing the number of oil-burning engines, changing over all the coal-burners to oil, and ordering oil-burners for all their new engines. Soon all the locomotives on the road will be equipped with oil-burners.

The Mining and Scientific Press, September 21, 1907.

BOSTON & ALBANY RAILROAD

An authority writes: "After an experience of a great many years in attempts to do away with black smoke from locomotives, I can say that Mr. Sinclair is absolutely correct in asserting that the firemen on locomotives can do more to eliminate black smoke than any smoke-consuming device ever invented."

SOUTHERN PACIFIC RAILROAD

We have been using liquid fuel on our locomotives for many years past, and now about all the engines in service are so equipped. The average cost of changing a coal-burning engine to liquid fuel is about $500. Through the use thereof, steam is more easily generated, and regulation of fire is under the absolute control of the fireman. Oil is used as fuel on our switch engines, as well as those operating in road service.

H. I. SMALL, General Superintendent Motive Power.

6. SMOKE TALK

MATERIAL AND VITAL COST

Chicago now derives a large income from fines imposed for violation of the smoke ordinances, and hundreds of furnaces are being annually changed to the smokeless types— and none too soon for the economical good of the city, for one of the great department store merchants on State street has made the statement that his annual loss because of goods being soiled by smoke amounted to nearly $200,000; that of State street, $2,000,000, and the total loss to the city occasioned by black smoke equaled the total of taxes paid by the city.

He does not estimate the total of deaths from tuberculosis, nor the number of sallow-faced, cellar-grown, oxygen-starved weaklings—men, women and children in Chicago's vast army of wealth-producing toilers, whose potentiality has been so sadly diminished from this same smoke.

According to a recent Berlin consular report, "One of the scientists at the London conference stated as a result of his analysis that between 500,000 and 1,000,000 tons of sulphuric acid were produced by the consumption of 16,000,000 tons of coal used annually in that city. Citizens are familiar with the effect of the acid on the respiratory organs. Its damage is visible on buildings, iron surfaces and public monuments. The Prussian government pays traveling instructors to educate men who have charge of furnaces."

SENTIMENT OR BUSINESS

"The two questions which gave us the most valued information were prompted by a desire to know just how the

manufacturers and other erstwhile offenders felt about it.
The first of these questions was:

"'*Do you consider that in making this installation of a
smoke-preventing device you have made a sacrifice to public
sentiment?*'

"To this question thirty-two replied 'no,' and of ten who
said 'yes,' only five were using mechanical stokers.

"The other question was:

"'*Do you consider that the good accomplished in smoke
abatement is worth the cost to manufacturers, hotels, etc.?*'

"Thirty-two said 'yes'; two said 'no,' and six were in doubt."

*Report upon Smoke Abatement,
Syracuse, N. Y., Chamber of Commerce, 1907.

SMOKE AND THE "OPEN TOWN"

Smoke lays tribute upon every householder by making
his family living more costly, and compelling him, if of limited
means, to economize where it were better that he should be
generous. Everything which purifies mind and morals costs
more in the dirty town than in the clean town. And the advocate of law-breaking, because it brings in money is, in truth,
an advocate of driving out of town much that legitimately
encourages expenditure. The modern city is inviting for homes
and for visiting when it has most to show of beauty and taste-
fulness. The "open town" man is indifferent to all such
considerations; to make one soiled dollar he destroys ten clean
dollars.

GEORGE A. THAYER, in "The Citizens' Bulletin."

THE COST IN ST. LOUIS

The smoke nuisance costs St. Louis more than $6,000,000
a year in damage to property of various kinds and in the
estimated amount that might be saved by smokeless gas-
producer plants. The librarian of the public library estimates
the damages by smoke to the books belonging to the public
at $10,000 annually.

Mr. Meyer says: "During the fiscal year of 1905–06 actual
figures show that the amount of dead trees cut down in Forest
Park was equivalent to 5.4 per cent of the entire number.
In my opinion about three-fourths of the foregoing percentage,

*This is one of the most comprehensive reports thus far issued,
on this subject, and will well repay a very careful study.

"WELL, THERE IT IS, MY PLAN FOR THE 'CITY BEAUTIFUL. "

"THAT MUST BE THE COMMITTEE. I FINISHED IT JUST IN TIME."

"THERE, GENTLEMEN, IS THE WAY CHICAGO WILL LOOK WHEN OUR IDEAS FOR ITS
BEAUTIFICATION ARE CARRIED OUT."

—Chicago Record-Herald

or namely, 4.05 per cent of the loss, can be attributed to the
effects of sulphuric gases from smoke."

Report of the Smoke Abatement Committee of
the Civic League, St. Louis, November, 1906.

THE ECONOMY OF SMOKELESS COMBUSTION

Illustrating the saving of fuel and the abatement of smoke
by the introduction of mechanical stokers: The Springfield

Brewing Company, of Springfield, Mo., has effected a saving of 50 per cent in fuel, the cost of smokelessly making steam from 1,000 pounds of water with Weir City slack at $1.90 per ton being 11.1 cents. The plant has one Heine boiler of 175 horse-power, and two return-tubular boilers of 100 horse-power each. The steamship "Eugene Zimmerman," of 10,000 tons rating, shows the smokeless working of two 263 horse-power internally-fired boilers. This ship runs between Duluth and lower Lake Erie ports and on the round trip uses 225 tons to 300 tons.

PAUL M. CHAMBERLAIN, Chief Engineer,
Under-feed Stoker Company of America.

THE CRIME OF THE CITY

The huge and ever-increasing cities, the vast manufacturing towns belching forth smoke and poisonous gases, with the crowded dwellings where millions are forced to live under the most terribly unsanitary conditions, are witnesses to a criminal apathy, an incredible recklessness and inhumanity. Yet, this is the one great and primary essential of a people's health and well-being, to which everything should for the time be subordinate.

DR. RUSSELL WALLACE, in his recent book,
"Man's Place in the Universe."

7. THE INTERNATIONAL ASSOCIATION FOR THE PREVENTION OF SMOKE

The following statements made by smoke inspectors at the Second Annual Convention of the International Association for the Prevention of Smoke, held at Milwaukee, June, 1907, are of great value, as representing the judgment and views of men with practical experience and charged with the special duty of smoke abatement.

"Ignorant firemen can destroy the value of the best smoke-preventing appliances."

"One concern saved from 10 to 15 per cent in fuel bills by paying the firemen four dollars per month premium if they prevented smoke. After that there was no complaint of smoke in that plant, which previously had proven a nuisance to the neighborhood. No changes had been made in the method of firing. The extra pay stopped the smoke and created a saving in the fuel bills greater than the premium paid the firemen."

"If ordinances were enacted to prosecute the owners of plants, engineers, firemen, and every one held responsible for smoke prevention in a steam plant, and the acts enforced, smoke would be abated immediately."

"No smoke-preventing appliance has been invented which does not require careful watching and intelligent operation. The best appliances are rendered useless by carelessness of owners and firemen."

"A smoking stack means a waste of money. Dividends are ushered out through the smoke stack as readily as they are in any other department of a manufacturing establishment."

"Cities and towns in Illinois, Ohio, Indiana and Michigan are taking the lead in smoke prevention."

"Railroads in the middle West, in seeking to prevent smoke from locomotives, have decreased their fuel bills considerably. As a result, some railroads engage their own inspectors, who watch the firing and report offenders. Firemen reported permitting smoke are laid off for various periods, from two to thirty days, and the second sentence usually stops the smoke nuisance on these railroads."

L. P. Breckenridge, Professor of Mechanical Engineering at the University of Illinois, said that boilers can be so arranged that there will be absolutely no smoke.

Smoke Inspector Schubert, of Chicago, said there is more than one million dollars worth of work being done in Chicago to improve conditions and to prevent smoke.

"Locomotives traveling in and out of Cleveland are not permitted to emit smoke."

"The New York Central is placing these perfection burners on all their locomotives and, on a careful test they made, found a saving of 12 per cent in fuel."

"The Pennsylvania railroad is carrying on experiments to carry the smoke at the roundhouse off into the sewers by throwing a spray of water over it."

"Fresh coal must not be added to the fire until the black gas from the previous coaling has passed off."

8. BIBLIOGRAPHY

Smoke literature is abundant, and no one need remain in ignorance unless determined to. The Department of Public Nuisances, American Civic Association, will be glad to give further information, but a consultation of the publications referred to below will fully illuminate those who care to let the light in.

Smoke Abatement. By Wm. Nicholson. J. B. Lippincott Company, 1905. $1.50.

Report upon Smoke Abatement. Chamber of Commerce Committee, Syracuse, N. Y., 1907. 42 pages.

Study of 400 Boiler Tests. United States Geological Survey, Washington, D. C.

Report on the Smoke Nuisance. By Z. A. Willard, Boston, 1907. 18 pages.

Publicity Magazine. The Under-feed Stoker Company of America, Chicago.

Smoke Prevention and Economy. Department of Smoke Abatement, Cleveland, Ohio, 1905.

Letters to Members. Anti-Smoke League, 213 St. Paul street, Baltimore, Md.

The Smoke Nuisance. American Civic Association, Washington, D. C., 1908. Second edition, 1911. This publication.

The Smoke Nuisance. Testimony collected from letters and interviews. Edwin R. Warren and others, Boston, 1905.

Smoke is Unnecessary. Extracts from letters, text books, 1905, reports and interviews, Edwin R. Warren and others, Boston.

Smoke and its Abatement. By Charles H. Benjamin, Cleveland, Ohio. In Vol. XXVI, American Society of Mechanical Engineers, 1905.

Smoke Prevention References to Books and Magazine Articles, May, 1907. Carnegie Library, Pittsburg, Pa. This bulletin is a very complete index and should be consulted by all who are interested in the subject.

The Burning of Coal Without Smoke in Boiler Plants. By D. T. Randall, United States Geological Survey, 1908.

Report Upon Smoke Abatement. Syracuse Chamber of Commerce, 1907.

How to Burn Illinois Coal Without Smoke. By L. P. Breckenridge, University of Illinois, 1907

Individuals and concerns, or city officials, taking up or advancing smoke prevention work are urged to communicate with the American Civic Association, Union Trust Building, Washington, D. C., and to give, for general help and encouragement, all possible information.

ND - #0248 - 080424 - C0 - 229/152/3 - PB - 9781332240739 - Gloss Lamination